DIY H

Brewing for Beginners

Everything You Need To Know

On How To Brew Awesome Beer

(Beginner Recipes Included)

Erich M. Tolman

Table of Contents

Bluesource And Friends

This book is brought to you by Bluesource And Friends, a happy book publishing company.

Our motto is **"Happiness Within Pages"**

We promise to deliver amazing value to readers with our books.

We also appreciate honest book reviews from our readers.

Connect with us on our Facebook page www.facebook.com/bluesourceandfriends and stay tuned to our latest book promotions and free giveaways.

DIY Home Beer Brewing For Beginners

Don't forget to claim your FREE books!

Brain Teasers:

https://tinyurl.com/karenbrainteasers

Harry Potter Trivia:

https://tinyurl.com/wizardworldtrivia

Sherlock Puzzle Book (Volume 2)

https://tinyurl.com/Sherlockpuzzlebook2

Also check out our best seller book

https://tinyurl.com/lateralthinkingpuzzles

Introduction

If you're reading this book, then you probably enjoy drinking good beer. Who doesn't? For you though, it's more than just simple enjoyment. If you're reading this book, it means that you want to know how it all works. You want to learn enough about beer that you'll be able to brew your own.

Where do you start? Well, first, let's examine the four main ingredients: water, barley, hops, and yeast. That sounds simple enough. But how does a brewmaster take these four basic ingredients, and turn them into something complex and flavorful?

Before that question can be answered, you must understand the basic purpose of each of those ingredients. First is the water. The water is what the entire beer will be built on. But did you know that the source of the water can change the taste of our beer?

DIY Home Beer Brewing For Beginners

Before a brewmaster can even begin to consider other ingredients, he must first look carefully at the source of his water.

The next ingredient is barley. Barley seems like such a simple plant, but we use it for so many things. It's in our cereal, our bread, and we use it to feed our animals. The way that we prepare our barley will determine the color and flavor of our beer. It also provides the sugars so that the yeast can work its magic and create alcohol.

Speaking of yeast, did you know that there are more than 1,500 species of yeast? If you were going to brew beer, which type of yeast would you choose? Could you justify your answer? Most of us probably couldn't. Even though we've been using yeast for cooking and brewing for thousands of years, there is still so much we don't know about it. Our best bet is to learn from the trial and error of brewers who have come before us.

It seems like nowadays, everyone is caught up on hops. But people were brewing beer for hundreds of years before anyone thought about adding hops. Modern brewers now add hops to give the beer that bitter and aromatic flavor that we love. When hops were first added to beer, it wasn't because of the flavor. You'll soon learn why we stopped making beer from just grain and water, and why we started adding that deliciously bitter smelling plant.

If you walked into any brewery or supermarket, you will see many kinds of beer. Take IPAs, for example. You might have hundreds of IPAs to choose from at the supermarket. But what makes one kind of IPA different from another?

DIY Home Beer Brewing For Beginners

There is historic and scientific precedence for the way that we brew our beer. Brewing is amazing because it is just as much a science as it is an art. The science that we understand about yeast and fermentation are open for experimentation with different kinds of ingredients, and while the science is the same, we can change the scientific process in order to alter the flavor of the beer we want to create.

When you have finished reading this book, you should have a basic understanding of the science and creativity that goes into making beer. Hopefully, you will have enough knowledge to begin brewing your own.

A Brief History of Beer

Beer is one of the oldest beverages in the world. It is difficult to trace its origins to one specific place. It has evolved independently in many different cultures throughout the world. The kind of beer that a culture makes is dependent upon what ingredients are available. Ancient Chinese beer makers used rice to make beer. European beer makers made beer out of different kinds of barley and wheat. In parts of Africa, sorghum was used as base malt. The grain in each place was different, but the beverage that became known as the beer had enough commonalities and was essentially brewed in the same way.

The oldest known beer is believed to be from around 7,000 to 5,000 BC in Iran. The oldest surviving beer recipe, written on a stone tablet from ancient Mesopotamia, is around 4,000 years old. There are even references to beer in the timeless Epic of Gilgamesh, written around 2100 BC when the

DIY Home Beer Brewing For Beginners

character Gilgamesh "ate until he was full, drank seven pitchers of beer, his heart grew light, his face flowed, and he sang out with joy." Villages in China may have been brewing beer as far back as 7,000 years. It's even referenced in Ancient Rome.

North African Tablets with beer recipes date back to 2,500 years BC. The ancient Greeks made barley wine: a very dark kind of ale that can be as high as 12% ABV. Even Native Americans brewed beer with corn and tree sap.

Before brewing became a major industry, people used spent grain to make beer for themselves. Beer brewing interestingly enough began in people's homes. It was another way of getting calories, and beer has always been enjoyed during celebrations. It was sometimes sold on a small scale from person to person, but it was mostly made and enjoyed domestically on a small scale.

DIY Home Beer Brewing For Beginners

Beer came shortly after the domestication of grain. When people discovered that grain was useful for food and began to plant it and tend to it, they quickly realized that they could make a simple fermented beverage from it. This was how the most basic form of beer came to be.

People began adding hops to their beer sometime in the 9th century when they discovered that it would help the beer last longer. People in Europe began to experiment with how much hops should be added to the beer. They found that if they added too much, the beer would be too bitter. But with just enough hops, the beer took on more flavors. Hops not only made the beer taste better, but it lasted longer, which made it possible to export and trade. With the implementation of hops, it could be carried for long distances. Beer eventually had commercial value, rather than just something that people brewed at home for themselves. It was a money-making tool. Popular beers like Indian Pale Ales got their name because they were brewed to last over long distances in ships headed for India and the Americas.

In the 14th and 15th centuries, the first dedicated breweries began to emerge. They were typically held in pubs and monasteries where beer was made and sold to go with food, or to raise money for the church. Trappist style beers come from monastic beer traditions where beer has been brewed in monasteries and abbeys for as long as 800 years.

During the industrial revolution, beer began to take on a form that we are familiar with today. Beer went from being an artisanal beverage to large-scale industry. Large amounts of beer could be produced in each batch. There were two important inventions that made the industrialization of beer possible.

DIY Home Beer Brewing For Beginners

The first important invention was the waterproof thermometer. The waterproof thermometer allowed brewing companies to maintain standard temperatures throughout the brewing process.

The second important tool is called a hydrometer. A hydrometer measures the final gravity of the beer. Gravity is the density of the beer, measured in relation to the density of water. Density is caused by malts or grains dissolving into the beer. These solids are the raw materials that yeast will convert into alcohol.

With a hydrometer, brewers could experiment with mixing malts and grains to affect flavor. By measuring the final gravity and mixing grains, they could create a beer that was high in alcohol content while using less grain and subsequently cutting costs. The hydrometer allowed brewers to see how each malt would affect the final gravity. Large commercial brewing operations began to emerge across the country, especially after the end of prohibition. Not much has changed. You will see that a thermometer and a hydrometer are still listed in this book as essential brewing equipment.

In the 1970s, the craft beer movement began. In 1978, Homebrewing became legal. This meant that anyone with the right tools and ingredients could brew up to 50 gallons of their own beer each year. You could say that brewing beer has come full circle. What began as a domestic practice in ancient times, and became a large-scale industry, has circled back around and is being practiced as a hobby by people all over the world.

People have been enjoying beer for thousands of years. As of writing this book, it is still the most preferred beverage in America. In 2019, the average person in the US drinks about 28 gallons of beer per year. Homebrewing has made a comeback, and craft beer culture has taken off. There are now about 4,000 craft breweries in the United States producing 15.6 million barrels of beer each year.

Chapter 1: Important Details and Beer Brewing Terms

Before you start to brew your own beer, try and think about which kinds of beer you enjoy the most. Maybe, sip your favorite amber or porter while you read this book, and think about what kind of beer you would like to make. If you aren't drinking beer yet, you will be craving it as soon as you start to learn about hops and barley.

Brewing is truly an art form that can take a whole lifetime to perfect. Some people focus on one type of beer and get really good at that. If you are reading this book, then you probably won't mind sampling new beers and trying new recipes. There are loads of resources out there about homebrewing, with entire books dedicated to just one or two styles of beer.

DIY Home Beer Brewing For Beginners

There are many terms that will be used within this book that have meanings that are specific to brewing. Before you begin reading about the process of brewing, it is important to familiarize yourself with these terms as they will be referenced and revisited in nearly every chapter. This list of definitions is very concise, but it will at least give you something to refer to when you see a word you don't recognize.

All-grain. The process used by experienced brewers uses to extract starches from malt by crushing it and then letting it sit in water at a high temperature. Most beginners save time by skipping this process and using an extract.

Aroma hops. Hops that are added to beer for the aromatic characteristics rather than for flavor.

DIY Home Beer Brewing For Beginners

Barley. A type of cereal grain that is often used in beer. One of the first domesticated grains.

Bitterness. Measured by the International Bitter Units scale, often abbreviated at IBU.

Bittering hops. Hops that are added to beer for their bittering characteristics. These types of hops are especially important for the overall flavor of a beer and have more alpha acids that aroma hops.

Fermentation. The process by which yeast breaks down sugars and turns them into alcohol.

Final gravity. The gravity of your beer when it has finished fermenting.

DIY Home Beer Brewing For Beginners

Gravity. This is the measure of the density of your wort or beer. It is a measured density relative to the density of water.

Hops. A flowering, leafy plant that grows on long vines. Added to beer because of its preservation qualities and for the bitter flavors and aromas that it adds.

International Bittering Units (IBU) Stands for International Bittering Units. A measure of the bitterness of the beer.

Malt. One of the main ingredients in beer. It is a grain that is kilned to release the sugars necessary for fermenting. Typically made from barley, but it can also be done using wheat, rye, or oat.

DIY Home Beer Brewing For Beginners

Original gravity. The gravity of the wort before you begin fermentation.

Pitching. Adding yeast to the wort at the start of the fermentation process.

Wort. This is what you call your beer before it starts fermenting. When you start to add your grains and your malts to the water, the water is no longer water; it is wort. Wort becomes beer the instant you add yeast. It may not be drinkable at this point, but this is how the phases are defined.

Yeast. A single-celled organism classified as a fungus that is responsible for the fermentation process. Yeast consumes sugar and excretes alcohol.

Chapter 2: Fermentation Process

The actual amount of time that your beer will need to ferment depends on the style and ingredients you have chosen. Still, the basic process will be more or less the same across the board.

Most beers can be fermented at around room temperate or just below at about 60-79 degrees Fahrenheit. Some beers require lagering. These beers are called lagers. Lagers are fermented at a lower temperature which slows down the rate of fermentation. It is possible to make these kinds of beers at home on a small scale. But lagering at a higher scale requires special refrigeration techniques that most home refrigerators are not capable of. All of the recipes in this book are possible to ferment at room temperatures.

DIY Home Beer Brewing For Beginners

The three stages of fermentation are primary, secondary, and conditioning. Each stage requires a separate container. Secondary fermentation is not necessary for all types of beer. For some, it is optional.

Primary fermentation happens after you make your wort. Your wort will be hot after you steep the grains and add the malts. This temperature is too high for the yeast to grow and survive. So, you have to cool your wort to around room temperature before the fermenting process can begin. For Homebrewing, the simplest method is to fill a sink or a tub with cold water and ice and place the pot of wort in the cold water. It is important to cool the wort as quickly as possible so that unwanted bacteria don't grow.

Next, you'll siphon the wort out of the pot and into a sanitized bucket. This is the bucket where primary fermentation will occur. It's important that your

DIY Home Beer Brewing For Beginners

bucket is airtight but still allows for CO_2 to escape. Once your wort is cooled and you've got it in the bucket, it's time to test the original gravity. Remember that the gravity is the density of your beer or wort relative to the density of water. The gravity of your beer is likely to change during fermentation as the yeast breaks down the sugars from the grain. Check the gravity by filling a hydrometer with some of your beer and watching to see how high the measure floats inside the hydrometer. Write down the original gravity to make sure that it matches with what the recipe calls for. You might need to add more water at this point in order to make adjustments to the density and volume of the beer.

After you have an original gravity reading, pitch your yeast. There are many different kinds of yeast and the kind you choose will depend on the type of beer you're making. Most yeast comes in dehydrated packets; sometimes it will require activation with

DIY Home Beer Brewing For Beginners

water. The yeast packet should have instructions.
Once the yeast is pitched, use a sanitized mixing tool
to make sure that it is adequately spread through the
wort. Now, seal the top of the bucket with the lid and
airlock/bubbler. You have started primary
fermentation.

Primary fermentation will account for the majority of
the alcohol content in the final beer. The conditions
in your wort and the sugars available create the
perfect environment for the yeast to produce and
consume like crazy. Yeast will consume all of the
oxygen in the bucket, and they'll start to put off CO_2
and alcohol. Check your airlock bubbler within a day
or two. You should see bubbles beginning to appear.
This is how you know that fermentation has started.
Your yeast is producing alcohol. The primary
fermentation state will last anywhere from a few days
to about a week depending on the malts and the yeast

in your beer. Refer to the recipe for specific instructions pertaining to your beer.

The next phase is the secondary fermentation. Most of the sugars have been converted by the yeast into ethanol, so fermentation begins to slow down quite a bit. The high level of alcohol in the wort is now making it harder for the yeast to continue to reproduce. Spent yeast begins to build up at the bottom of the fermenting container, so we need to get rid of that in order for fermentation to continue. To begin secondary fermentation, we'll siphon the beer into a new container. It should be similar to the first container; a fermentation bucket or a glass carboy that allows CO_2 to escape but won't let any air in. Secondary fermentation will last one or two weeks and is typically longer because, by this time, fermentation has slowed down significantly. Secondary fermentation will help the beer look clearer and have less sediment. It is also important to remove

DIY Home Beer Brewing For Beginners

the old yeast because it can affect the final flavor of the beer.

The third stage of fermenting is called conditioning. You'll once again need to move the beer into a new container. But the third container will be whatever you enjoy your beer out of. Whether you choose to put your beer in a keg or in bottles, this is where conditioning will happen. Later on, in this book, we will discuss the pros and cons of putting your beer in bottles or kegs. For now, though, we'll just talk about what conditioning is and why it important.

Conditioning, to explain it in the simplest way, is necessary for the beer to have carbonation. If we didn't condition our beer, it would be flat. Let's assume that we'll be using bottles. At this stage, our beer is still in the secondary fermentation bucket. By now, almost all of the sugars have been consumed by the yeast, and the yeast is desperate for something to consume. Before conditioning, we will add a small amount of priming sugar, which looks a lot like normal sugar, to our wort. This will give the yeast something new to feast on, and it will start to produce more CO2.

Once you've added the priming sugar, move the beer into sanitized bottles. You could also place the beer in kegs. The amount of time that is necessary for the beer to condition will depend on the place. Store your beer in a cool, dark place for a week or two. The yeast will consume all of the oxygen and sugar in the beer during that time, and the CO_2 that it gives off will give your beer carbonation.

Chapter 3: Equipment Needed

From reading through the last chapter, you might be starting to think that this new hobby will require all kinds of equipment, like fermenting buckets and fancy pots for boiling your wort. Don't be intimidated. You can get started with basic equipment for about 150 dollars. Many cities in the US have homebrewing supply stores. If you aren't lucky enough to have a homebrewing store in your home town, you can turn to the internet for your equipment and ingredients. You can buy kits that include all the parts you'll need. These kinds of kits can be found online and usually run between 100 and 200 bucks. These will give you everything you need to get started, and they may even include a free recipe book. Some homebrewing kits also include enough ingredients to get you started on your first beer.

Most of the brewing kits in this price range will have the same equipment, more or less. If you're curious,

DIY Home Beer Brewing For Beginners

you can do a little research. But I've provided a comprehensive list of the basic equipment that you'll want to have, plus a handful of extra items that are relatively inexpensive upgrades, but you'll find that the investment is worth it if you decide to keep making beer and you want the process to be as user-friendly as possible.

Basic Homebrewing Supplies

A big pot. The bigger your pot is, the better. It needs to be able to hold at least 4 gallons. You'll use this to boil your wort and steep your grains. *$25-30.*

Two six-gallon plastic buckets with spigot or glass carboys. Plus, a lid with a hole drilled in it for the airlock. If you have two of these buckets, you will have an easier time with secondary fermentation. Most food quality plastic buckets will work, as long as you can sanitize them. *$15-40 each.*

DIY Home Beer Brewing For Beginners

Airlock and stopper. This is probably the most 'high tech' piece of equipment for homebrewing, and they are pretty simple. You put a little bit of water in the airlock and it sits on top of your fermenting bucket. CO_2 escapes in bubbles through the water, but it keeps air from getting in. *$3-6 each.*

Burlap or nylon bags. You'll fill these bags with grain or hops and steep them in hot water to make wort.

Racking can or siphon. You'll use this several times throughout the brewing process. Having a siphon will help keep sediment out of your beer when you move your wort from the pot after boiling, and when you go between different fermenting stages and conditioning. *$15.*

DIY Home Beer Brewing For Beginners

Food safe iodine or acidic, no-rinse sanitizer. It's important to keep all of your equipment well-sanitized throughout the brewing process. *$6 for 4oz.*

Hydrometer and jar. Used for measuring the gravity of your wort and beer. *$15.*

Waterproof thermometer. Critical for maintaining a stable temperature throughout the process of steeping grain and making wort. *$15.*

Bottle caps and capper. For sealing your delicious home-brewed beer into airtight bottles at the beginning of the conditioning process. *$10-15.*

Bottling wand. For measuring and moving your beer into bottles. *$10.*

DIY Home Beer Brewing For Beginners

5 ft 3/8-inch beverage tubing. Attach this to the siphon for running your wort into the primary fermenter and moving your beer from the primary fermentation bucket into the secondary fermentation bucket.

Bottles. You can order these online or buy them from breweries or brewing supply stores. Try your local brewery, as they can often be supportive places for local brewing culture. Gather a bunch of bottles for free by throwing a party and saving all the bottles. Brown bottles work the best for keeping light out. Keep in mind a standard 5-gallon batch will require about 48 bottles.

Homebrewing on the basic level doesn't actually require too much equipment as far as hobbies go. For an investment of about $150, you can have a fun new weekend hobby, not to mention all of the great beer you'll be making. It's not too expensive, and there are

DIY Home Beer Brewing For Beginners

tons of free resources, recipes, and brewing forums online to keep you busy and experimenting. Homebrewing forums are an excellent place to compare notes on gear and ingredients.

Below is a list of equipment that may be too expensive when you are first starting, but you will probably want them if you brew more than one or two batches of beer. They'll make the brewing process faster and easier, and your beer more professional.

Other Homebrewing Equipment

Glass carboys. These were already listed up above next to fermenting buckets. You can get this right away for fermenting your beer rather than using plastic buckets. Glass is easier to sanitize. Some home brewers swear by glass carboys, insisting that it has an impact on flavor. They are typically more expensive than plastic buckets, but it's worth the investment. $30.

Wort chiller. Lowering the temperature of your wort as quickly as possible will help keep your wort from getting unwanted bacteria. You can use a bathtub, or a sink filled with ice cold water, but this process is slow if your batch is big. A wort chiller is made of coiled copper. After you finish boiling your wort, you place the wort chiller inside your wort and run cold water through it. It carries away the heat of the wort and can bring boiling wort down to room temperature within a few minutes. $60.

Kettle. These will typically work better than your standard stove pot and can hold higher quantities of wort. Many have false bottoms and built-in thermometers to help maintain a more consistent temperature during boiling. $150.

DIY Home Beer Brewing For Beginners

Propane stove. The burner on your regular kitchen stove will work just fine but trying to bring five gallons of water to a boil on an electric stove can take a long time. Homebrewing supply companies make large, portable propane burners that can boil wort much faster. A good propane stove and a brewing kettle will make you brew like a pro. $150.

Chapter 4: Sanitation and Hygiene

Probably the most important part of brewing is keeping everything clean and sanitized. By putting fermentable sugars in water and leaving them for a few weeks, you are creating the perfect environment for even small amounts of bacteria to grow like crazy. This will ruin the taste of your beer.

A good home brewer will pay considerable attention to detail in keeping everything sanitized. Remember that yeast is bacteria, and that beer is essentially a result of growing the right bacteria. It's very easy to grow the wrong bacteria.

You need to sanitize everything that will touch the wort when it cools below 160 degrees. This includes your Fermenter and all of its pieces including the

DIY Home Beer Brewing For Beginners

airlock funnel and siphon. You also need to sanitize your thermometer, fermenter lid, yeast starter jar, and anything you will use for mixing the yeast into the wort. It's not enough to just wash your equipment the same way you would wash dishes.

Different Methods of Sanitizing

Bleach

Use 1 tablespoon of bleach per one gallon of water. Soak everything in this mixture for 20 minutes and then drain. You don't need to rinse, but some brewers insist on rinsing with boiled water to remove the chances of odd flavors from the chlorine.

Star San

Star San is an acid designed specifically for Homebrewing. It's a favorite for many home brewers. Take 1oz of Star San for every 5 gallons of water.

DIY Home Beer Brewing For Beginners

Your equipment only needs to soak for 30 seconds, and there is no need to rinse. To make it easier, you can fill a couple of spray bottles with the concoction and spray your brewing equipment down before you use it. It is less harmful than bleach.

Iodophor

To use Iodophor, soak one tablespoon per 5 gallons of water. Leave your equipment soaking for two minutes. Iodophor is brown and comes in a bottle with its own measuring device. It can stain plastic, but it won't affect the flavor of your beer.

Even the bottle you use for condition needs to be cleaned and sanitized. The best way to clean your bottles is to use a scrub brush on the inside to remove all the debris, and then soak them in your bleach solution for a few hours.

Chapter 5: Choosing the Right Ingredients

Many first-time homebrewers will choose to brew beer using a kit. This is a good way to get your feet wet and practice the steps of boiling the wort and fermentation. But once you understand the process a little better, you'll want to start creating your own recipes. After all, brewing your own beer gives you the freedom to create what you want. But it's important to understand the different kinds of ingredients available and how each one will affect the flavor of your beer.

We've already established that beer is basically made of four ingredients: grain, hops, water, and yeast. But under each of these categories, there are many different variations that will produce different styles of beer. Below, we have listed several different kinds

DIY Home Beer Brewing For Beginners

of malt grains and hops that are popular and widely available for homebrewing. You can read about these different malts and hops and recognize that they all have different properties that you can experiment with. Brewers have been using these ingredients for years, and you find lots of information online about all of their flavor profiles. But you can use this book as a reference when you decide to start making your own recipes.

Malts

Malt may be the most important component of brewing beer. Even though hops are the most obvious part of a beer's flavor, grains and malts are critical for the color and flavor that the beer will have once it has been brewed and fermented. There are countless kinds of malts made from different types of common grain.

DIY Home Beer Brewing For Beginners

The word malt is used to describe a grain, usually barley that has been made into cereal and processed in such a way to release the sugars from the starches. Malt is a grain with water added so that the seeds begin to germinate. Then, they are roasted in order to affect the flavor and stop the growth. This process forces the grain to release sugars. If you are a home brewer, it may be easier to use barley that has already been processed into malt. Making your own malt from raw grain is done through a process called mashing. For most home brewers, they use a malt extract.

Malt can be bought in a few different forms, ready to go straight into your brew. It can come as both liquid malt extract and as dry malt extract. Dry malt extract is a powder made from dehydrated malt, while liquid malt extract comes in a thick liquid similar to the consistency of syrup or molasses. Most beers are made from a combination of many different kinds of malts. Liquid malt extract is typically easier to mix, but both are easy to use for homebrewing. Different kinds of malts will affect the beer's flavor differently, and most beers are made of a mix of several different kinds of malts.

Most malt is made from barley, but malts are also commonly made out of wheat and rye. The properties of barley make it ideal for brewing. Hordeum vulgaer, which is the scientific name for barley, comes from the Middle East and moved across Europe. It is now the 4th most common type of cereal grain. It's used to make whiskey, animal feed, and cereal. It grows in husks with kernels on the end of long grass, similar to corn. Barley that will be used to produce malt is held to an extremely high standard, because it is essential for it to be able to release the sugars and starches properly.

DIY Home Beer Brewing For Beginners

Brewing with an all-grain mix isn't necessarily better than malt extract brewing. Some homebrewing snobs will tell you that this will make better beer. But there are plenty of good malt extracts to choose from for all different styles of beer.

Making your own mash involves a process of getting the barley wet so that the seeds begin to germinate. Once they have started to germinate, they are put in a kiln and roasted. Heating them helps to start the process of converting the starches to sugars. Roasting the barley at different temperatures for different amounts of time will affect the flavor of the malt. The longer it is roasted and the hotter the kiln, the stronger the flavors will be. The advantage of making your own grains is the ability to make a malt have very specific flavors. Although there are many different kinds of extracts to mix and add to your beer, if you are very serious about brewing, you may wish to do your own mash so that you have more control over the final flavor and color of the beer. This kind of brewing is known as all-grain brewing. But you can make very good beer using just malt extracts, and there is nothing wrong with brewing your beer this way.

Even if you aren't brewing with all-grain, you can use different specialty grains to the impact flavor and color. Steep different grains in your wort as if you are making a giant cup of 'tea' made out of grain. The malt is what gives the yeast food to eat. The starches in barley are converted to sugars.

These grains are one of the easiest ways for a new brewer to experiment and mess around with flavor a bit. Heat up some water and steep different combinations of your specialty grains in it to experiment with different flavors. You don't need to go through the entire brewing process to try different combinations of flavors, which makes this a fun way to try different things in your brewing.

Some of the other common types of grains that are used in beer include rye, wheat, and oats. Barley still constitutes the majority of malts because of its properties, but most recipes combine different kinds of malt for flavor.

Wheat is the second most common type of grain used in beer. The husks on wheat are smaller. A compound called ester is what gives wheat its smells and flavor. Rye is malt that originated in Germany and is popular in many German styles of beer. It has a smoky, peppery flavor. Rye contains lots of protein and is typically used less than wheat and barley. Oats are another type of malt. They are rarely used except in stouts and porters.

DIY Home Beer Brewing For Beginners

The malts you choose to use will have the biggest impact on the color of the beer. People often think that a darker beer means a stronger beer, but this is not always a good indicator of the strength of the beer.

There is an official scale for the color of the beer. While it isn't as important if you are brewing for fun, it is good to know. The scale for the color of beer is measured in degrees Lovibond. The scale was developed by Joseph Lovibond in 1893. Degrees Lovibond is the most widely accepted scale of beer color in the US. A beer with a very light color is only a few degrees Lovibond. A wheat beer might be around 5 degrees Lovibond, while a Russian Imperial Stout might be upwards of 400 or 500 degrees Lovibond. It's not totally necessary to worry about degrees Lovibond when you are making beer at home, but it's good to use as a reference when you are choosing malts.

DIY Home Beer Brewing For Beginners

Below, we've listed a handful of common malts and their uses, in addition to a brief description of their flavor and color characteristics. Remember to consult different brewing forums if you are looking at creating a specific recipe. Most of these malts have been experimented with for a long time, and there is a lot of wisdom to be gained from the trial and error of people who have been brewing for a long time.

Common Base Malts

Base malts are malts that will make up the majority of a beer's malt profile. They are high in sugars and give the yeast a lot to feed on. This is what you will be using the most of in your beers.

Munich Malt

DIY Home Beer Brewing For Beginners

The Munich malt is malt that is high in enzymes, meaning that it has a lot of sugar for the yeast to break down. If you are using a Munich Malt, it will probably be the grain you are using the most of. It was developed in Munich in the 1830s at the Spaten Brewery. It works well in Oktoberfest style beers.

Pilsner Malt

While it is referred to as pilsner Malt, it has more uses than just pilsners. It is very light and has a high enzyme content, with a clean crisp taste made from two-row barley.

Pale Malt

Pale malt is very popular base malt, especially in ales. It can be made from either a two or six-row barley. It has a similar flavor and enzymatic properties to the pilsner, but it has a longer kiln time.

DIY Home Beer Brewing For Beginners

Maris Otter Malt

Maris Otter malt is English barley first created in 1966. It does well in ales that are slightly bitter or mildly bitter. It is a very picky type of barley, preferring certain climates. It grows especially well in England. It is a popular choice for both craft and home brewers. Many popular English ales use Maris Otter malt as a base.

Wheat Malt

Wheat malts are very light in flavor. If you think of your favorite wheat beer, it will likely have a similar flavor profile. Most wheat beers use a combination of wheat and barley malts. Most brewers strongly advise against using only wheat as malt, because it doesn't have the same essential enzymatic properties of barley. Malt made only out of barley can result in clogged wort, because it has so much protein. There aren't enough enzymes in wheat, so the starches don't convert to sugar properly.

Vienna Malt

If you were to measure the Vienna malt on a color scale, it would fall somewhere between pilsner malt and Munich malt. It can be used as base malt. It does well in Vienna lagers.

Mild Malt

Similar to the Maris Otter malt. It is made out of barley, with a nutty flavor. Just like the Marris Otter, it goes well in English ales.

Specialty Malts

DIY Home Beer Brewing For Beginners

Base malts will make up the majority of the malt profile for your beer, but specialty malts are added in small amounts to enhance the flavor and aroma of the final beer. They have lower enzymatic properties, which mean that there are fewer sugars available for the yeast to break down.

Aromatic Malt

The aromatic malt has a flavor that is reminiscent of a biscuit. It is left in the kiln for a long time at high temperatures, so it is very dark in color. It is commonly used in brown ales and bocks.

Crystal Malt

Crystal malt is clear malt that gives the beer a sweet flavor. There are different types of crystals malts that will result in different colors and different levels of sweetness. Crystal malt with a lower temperature and shorter kiln time will have a light sweetness, while crystal malt left in the kiln longer will be very rich. Crystal malts are unique because they are stewed after kilning.

Chocolate Malt

The chocolate malt is very dark, sitting between 300-400 degrees Lovibond. It will give your beer a dark chocolate flavor. If you are going to use this, only small amounts are necessary. If you add too much chocolate malt, it can give your beer a burnt taste.

Black Malt

The Black malt is even darker than chocolate malt. In fact, it is the darkest kind of malt. Because of its flavor, it's very important to use even less of it in your beer. A little bit will go a long way, and too much will make your beer taste bad. It is very popular in porters.

It has very poor enzymatic properties, which means there is hardly any fermentable sugar in it for the yeast to eat.

Smoked Malt

Rauchbier is a traditional kind of German beer that is known for its smoky flavor. Smoked malt is the ingredient that gives it this characteristic. Smoked malt is made in a kiln that is left exposed to the open flame, so that the smoke mixes with the grain while it malts. It does well in a Rauchbier as well as in smoked porters. It may also be found in popular scotch whiskeys. Despite its smoky flavor, it is actually lighter malt. It has very little enzymatic properties, which mean it doesn't provide much sugar for the yeast by itself.

Carapils

DIY Home Beer Brewing For Beginners

Carapils is a cross between caramel malt and pilsner malt. It is lighter in color. Carapils is often added to pale ales and lagers in small amounts. A bock will require more carapils to produce its flavor. It is known for giving the beer a good, foamy head.

Biscuit Malt

The biscuit malt is a kind of malt known for its distinct bready, or cracker-like, flavor. Like many of the other specialty malts, it does not do well as base malt because of its low enzymatic properties. The biscuit malt is common in brown ales.

Rye Malt

As the name would suggest, rye malt is commonly used in rye beers. A classic example of a rye beer would be the Roggenbier that comes from Bavaria. Rye faces many of the same problems that wheat will face when used as malt, so it is best to use it in small amounts as a specialty grain, rather than a base grain. It will give the beer a spicy flavor and is red in color.

Choosing the Right Yeast

When it comes to making good beer, yeast is our best ally. While we have creative control of all of the ingredients that we choose, the actual fermenting process is all left up to our yeast. When we pitch the yeast and seal our fermenting bucket, the fate of our beer is in the yeast's hands. The most important thing we can do is choose the right yeast and provide it with the best environment to multiply and produce alcohol.

Yeast is a single-celled organism called a eukaryote. It technically falls under the category of fungi. Brewing is only one of the jobs that yeast is useful for. It has literally hundreds of applications in the production of food and beverages. Yeast really should be considered

DIY Home Beer Brewing For Beginners

a friend. After all, without yeast, we wouldn't have alcohol. We know less about how yeast works than we do about all the other ingredients that go into beer.

Just as there are many types of hops and malts, there are hundreds of strains of yeast. Choosing the right kind of yeast is very important for the end product of your beer. Like the other aspects of homebrewing, don't get intimidated by the vast number of yeasts available for brewing. You won't need to know all of them when you are first starting out. Depending on the kind of beer that you choose to make, there is plenty of information available on the internet and from brewing forums about what kind of yeast is best suited for the job. This book could easily turn into a manual about different strains of yeast, so trying to list the 'important' types of yeast would be an impossible job, and it would be impractical for this introduction to brewing. Your best bet is to do some research on what kind of beer you are trying to make, and figure out what other people have used and what works.

Yeast can basically be split into two different categories. You can get more technical and argue that there are more categories, and you wouldn't be wrong. The more we learn, the harder it is to classify all the peculiarities of each strain. But for now, in order to gain a basic understanding, we will use these two categories.

The first category of yeast is called Saccharomyces cerevisiae. A more common way to remember that is to think of them as 'top-fermenting.' This means that the yeast will hang out on the top of your beer, and that is where they will ferment. Top-fermenters are typically used in ales, wheats, stouts, porters, and Kolsch beers. The top fermenting beers typically create a lot of foam at the head, and as a result, these styles of beer usually have more foam when you pour them. Top-fermenting yeast thrives at relatively higher temperatures, between 50-77 degrees Fahrenheit.

If the first category is called top-fermenters, then it follows that the next category contains your bottom-fermenters. The scientific name for bottom-fermenting yeast is Saccharomyces uvarum. They don't grow as quickly as top-fermenting yeasts. They actually prefer an environment that is a bit colder, between 45-60 degrees Fahrenheit. This type of yeast settles at the bottom of your fermenter. Just like with top-fermenters, the flavor of your beer will depend on what strain you use. But bottom-fermenters have less head and are common in lagers, pilsners, bocks, and American malts.

Now that you have at least a vague idea of how different types of yeast work, you can think about where to start your research. You'll see that almost every single recipe in this book requires a different kind of yeast specific to that beer. Most yeast packets only cost a few dollars and can be easily found online or in a homebrewing shop. If you are using a recipe, it should tell you exactly what kind of yeast to use. If you are trying to brew something of your own, for example, a pale ale, read up on how different kinds of yeast will interact with the malts you have chosen. There will be a lot of information and several different kinds of yeast to choose from for each style of beer.

Water

The first and most obvious ingredient in beer is water. Without water, there would be nothing to steep our grains in, and we wouldn't have anywhere for our yeast to live and grow. The topic of how water will affect our beer is a rabbit hole, and there are as many opinions as there are people brewing beer. This is largely due to the fact that your water source will have an effect on the flavor of your beer. But it is impossible to say that there is one type of water that is better than all of the others.

Water is a perfect example of what makes brewing so special. The water source chosen can have a distinctive effect on the style of beer. For example, Dortmund Germany is especially known for its famous pale lagers. You could attribute some of this success to the water, which has higher levels of chloride and helps to compliment the flavor of the malt. Dark beers tend to do better with harder water, while pales taste better with water that is slightly more acidic.

Most brewers believe that trying to keep your water somewhere between 5.2-5.5 on the pH scale is a safe bet. You can test the pH of your water to get it right. If you don't want to mess with your tap water, you can buy mountain spring water. It is widely accepted that mountain spring water is one of the best choices because of its low mineral content and purity.

Don't stress too much about the type of water that you choose. If your tap water is clean to drink, there is not much reason why you won't be able to create a good beer with it. Selecting the right water source is most important when you are trying to imitate a certain type of beer, like a Dortmund Pale Lager. There are a lot of details to remember when you are learning how to brew beer, so don't stress too much on all of these things at first. But it is definitely good to have in the back of your mind, especially if you plan on getting serious about brewing.

Hops

Hops seem to be the favorite ingredient for a lot of people. IPAs have risen in popularity in the United States, especially since the craft beer movement has taken off. Hops are responsible for the bitter flavor of the beer. If a beer tastes bitterer, we might call it 'hoppy.'

Humulus lupulus, commonly known as hops, have been bred for centuries in order to mix certain characteristics. The cone of the flower, called the strobile, is added to the wort near the end of the brewing process in order to add flavor, aroma, and preserve our beer. It is believed that hops first came from China, but they are grown across the world now with different countries and climates boasting their own unique varieties of hops.

As a plant, hops don't last very long. They quickly start to lose their oils and become spoiled after they are picked. Fresh hops can make for a fuller and fresher flavor, but they will most likely need to be preserved. In order for them to be preserved, they have to be dried and refrigerated to maintain their properties. Some breweries use fresh hops in their beer. For most homebrewers though, this is impractical. You will most likely be using hop pellets in your beer. There is nothing wrong with that. In fact, many craft breweries use hop pellets, and delicious beer can be made from dried and preserved hops. They are more concentrated and will last longer, which means we don't need to start a hop farm in order to brew our own beer. Growing hops could be another cool hobby, and it might be a cool addition to your garden.

Hops are a flower that can be male or female. Brewers use female hops for brewing. Hops have to be boiled in order for the oils and acids to be released into the beer. The bitterness in hops comes from the alpha acids, which are found in the oils in the leaves. Alpha acids are measured as a percentage of the oils in a given hop. To put it simply, the higher the percentage, the more bittering potential the hop has.

DIY Home Beer Brewing For Beginners

You can split hops into two main categories, and then a third category that lies somewhere in between. The category that a hop falls in is determined by the alpha acids present in the oils in the hop.

The first category consists of bittering hops. Bittering hops have a high percentage of alpha acids, sometimes over 20% alpha. These hops are responsible for the bitter flavor in a beer.

Aroma hops contain fewer alpha acids and oils, which means that they contribute less to the bitterness of the beer. Aroma hops are added because of the aroma they produce. They are usually somewhere between 3-4% alpha. The aroma also comes from the oils present in the hops.

The third category of hops consists of dual-purpose hops. Not all hops fall into just one category. Dual purpose hops are added to the beer because they can do both; giving the beer a good smell as well as helping to make the beer bitterer.

There is a pretty simple method of calculating the bitterness of the beer you are trying to create. This scale is measured by what is called Homebrew Bitterness Units (HBU). If you want to combine different kinds of hops, you can use the HBU as a reference for how much hops you will need to add.

The HBU is calculated using a very simple equation. Take the alpha acid percentage and multiply it by the number of ounces you want to add. If you plan to use 1.5 ounces of a 5.5% Brewers Gold bittering hop, then your beer will be 8.25 AAUs. If you decide to substitute one hop with another hop that has a different alpha percentage, you can use this to calculate how much of the replacement hop you will need. Keep in mind that this calculation only works

DIY Home Beer Brewing For Beginners

for hops that you will boil for 60 minutes in a 5-gallon batch.

Professional brewers use International Bittering Units (IBU). While HBU is useful for calculating the bitterness before you make your beer, IBU measures the actual bitterness of the finished beer. The IBU scale can account for different boiling times, different volumes of beer, different temperatures, and different gravities. This is why the IBU scale would be more useful if you are starting a commercial brewing operation. If you'd like to get an estimate of IBU for your beer, brewersfriend.com has a good estimator where you plug in all the relevant information and it calculates the IBU for you. Otherwise, the math is a little too involved for a basic book on homebrewing.

Bittering Hops

Admiral

DIY Home Beer Brewing For Beginners

Admiral hops are high in alpha acids, around 13-16% alpha. They were originally bred in England.

Flavor characteristics: citrus, wood, and herbs.

Substitute: Cascade.

Brewers Gold

Brewers Gold is a milder hop at around 5.5-7.8% alpha. First bred in 1919.

Flavor characteristics: mellow and spicy.

Substitutes: Northdown, Galena, Cascade, and Chinook.

Bullion

First bred in 1919. Sits around 10% alpha. An advantage of the Bullion hop is that it stores for a long time without spoiling. Used in various styles of beer.

DIY Home Beer Brewing For Beginners

Chinook

Chinook is a very strong, bitter hop at 12-14% alpha. It was first bred in 1985.

Flavor characteristics: spicy, pine, and herbs.

Substitutes: very bitter hops like Amarillo, Brewers Gold, and Target.

Galena

Developed in 1978. Another strong hop at 11.5-14% alpha.

Flavor characteristics: balanced bitter with a fruity aroma

Substitutes: Nugget and CTZ.

Eroica

DIY Home Beer Brewing For Beginners

The Eroica hop is relatively rare and highly sought after for specific types of beer. Eroica is another strong one, between 12-15% alpha.

Flavor characteristics: fruity.

Substitutes: Bullion, Galena, and Glacier.

Herald

It's best to use Herald in smaller amounts. Developed in England in the 1990s. A strong hop at 11.9-12.8% alpha.

Flavor characteristics: citrusy aroma.

Substitute: Pioneer.

Magnum

Magnum is not very aromatic, first created in Germany. Lingers around 12-14% alpha.

Substitute: Columbus, Nugget.

DIY Home Beer Brewing For Beginners

Nugget

An American at about 9.5%-14% alpha. Some might argue that it falls under the category of a dual-purpose hop.

Flavor characteristics: bitter and aromatic.

Substitute: Columbus, Tomahawk, Zeus.

Pacific Gem

Bred out of New Zealand at 13-16% alpha.

Flavor characteristics: berry aromas.

Substitute: CTZ.

Perle

Another hop that could fall in the category of dual purpose, developed in Germany in 1978. This hop can come in a wide range between 5.9-9.5% alpha. Good for German style beers.

Substitute: Northern Brewer.

Cluster

A very popular hop in American craft beer with a wide range of uses. Around 5.5-8% alpha.

Flavor characteristics: floral.

Columbus

Columbus is a very bitter hop at 14-18% alpha. Even when it is only used in low quantities. A popular choice for American IPAs.

Substitutes: Cascade, Chinook.

Pride of Ringwood

Bred in Australia at around 9-10.5% alpha. It is a very bitter hop.

Flavor characteristics: earthy and herbal.

Substitute: Millennium.

Sorachi Ace Japanese

Very popular in America and has a predictable flavor.

Flavor characteristics: citrus.

Substitute: Citra.

Warrior

This hop is very high in bitterness at 15-17% alpha.

Substitute: CTZ.

Dual Purpose Hops

DIY Home Beer Brewing For Beginners

<u>Amarillo</u>

A very popular hop. Bred in 2000 in Washington State. Alpha at 8-11%. Works for bittering but also a distinct aroma.

Substitute: Cascade, Chinook.

<u>Centennial</u>

Another hop from Washington State. It contains about 9.5-11.5% alpha.

Flavor characteristics: pine, grapefruit, and citrusy.

Substitute: Cascade, Chinook.

<u>Challenger</u>

An English hop developed in 1972 with 6.5-8.5% alpha.

Flavor characteristics: mellow fruit, spicy aroma.

DIY Home Beer Brewing For Beginners

Substitute: Perle, Northern Brewer.

Citra

American hop that is popular for IPAs and has good bittering qualities at 10-12% alpha.

Flavor characteristics: fruity and citrusy.

Substitute: Simcoe, Amarillo

Progress

Developed in the 1950s in England with 5-7% alpha.

Flavor characteristics: berry aromas.

Horizon

10.2-16.5% alpha.

Flavor characteristics: floral aroma.

Substitute: Magnum.

DIY Home Beer Brewing For Beginners

Northern Brewer

Developed in 1934, Northern Brewer is mostly used for bittering but has a good aroma.

Mt Hood

Mt Hood is a hop that is very popular in America. It was bred in 1983 and is 5-8% alpha.

Flavor characteristics: very spicy aroma good for bittering as well.

Sterling

Developed at Oregon State. This hop can have a high range and can be anywhere from 4.5-9% alpha. Does well in German and Czech Lagers.

Flavor characteristics: citrus and pine.

Substitute: Saaz, Mt Hood.

DIY Home Beer Brewing For Beginners

<u>Target</u>

At 11% alpha, target is used mostly for bittering. It doesn't last as long, so the freshness of this hop is essential.

Flavor characteristics: floral aroma.

Substitutes: Fuggle, Willamette.

Aroma Hops

<u>Cascade</u>

A hop that is very popular in American craft beer. It's about 4.5-5% alpha.

Aroma characteristics: citrus and pine.

Substitutes: Amarillo, Centennial.

<u>East Kent Goldings</u>

Popular in English Ales.

DIY Home Beer Brewing For Beginners

Aroma characteristics: floral, mellow, and a little bitter.

Substitutes: Fuggle, Kent Goldings.

<u>Fuggle</u>

Developed in 1875 by Richard Fuggle. Primarily used in English style ales.

<u>Hallertauer Hersbrucker</u>

Works well in Pilsners.

Aroma characteristics: grassy and floral.

Substitutes: Hallertauer Mittlefrueh, Liberty.

<u>Hallertauer Mittlefrueh</u>

A German hop that typically has small yields and is susceptible to plant diseases.

Aroma characteristics: spice and herb aroma.

Substitutes: Liberty, Mt Hood.

Liberty

Similar to Hallertauer Mittlefrueh but grows better and is less susceptible to disease.

Not as aromatic but has some similar characteristics. Around 3-6% alpha. The freshness of this hop is important.

Aroma characteristics: vanilla.

Substitutes: Hallertauer Mittlefrueh, Mt Hood.

Saaz

Does well in Bohemian pilsners and Czech beers. Saaz is about 3-5% alpha.

Aroma characteristics: a little bitter.

DIY Home Beer Brewing For Beginners

Substitutes: Sterling, Tettnanger, Spalt.

Santiam

American, very similar to Tettnanger. It was first bred in Oregon and is about 5-8% alpha. Works well in pilsners, Kolschs.

Aroma characteristics: clean and crisp aroma.

Spalt

Does well in German and Czech style beers.

Aroma characteristics: spicy.

Substitutes: Hallertauer Hersbrucker, Saaz.

Tettnanger:

A German hop very similar to Saaz. It's about 2.5-5.5% alpha.

Aroma characteristics: earthy and citrusy.

Substitute: Saaz

Willamette

An American developed in the 1970s at Oregon State. It can be used in a variety of beers. It's about 4-8% alpha.

Aroma characteristics: spicy aroma.

Substitutes: Fuggle, Tettnanger.

Chapter 6: Bottling And Kegging

Whether you put your beer in kegs or bottles, this will ultimately determine where you will end up conditioning your beer. Recall that conditioning is the step after secondary fermentation, where we add sugar and move our beer out of the fermenter and into kegs or bottles. This step is essential for creating carbonation.

Not only is this where your beer will be conditioned, but this is also what you will serve your beer out of. Special equipment is required for kegging, which we will list below. The process of bottling is much simpler and costs less. Kegging is more expensive but results in better beer. Most home brewers will choose to bottle their beer for the first couple of times. It works well for small batches and it's relatively easy. Bottles are also smaller than kegs, so storage is easier.

DIY Home Beer Brewing For Beginners

It's easier to keep your beers cold in the fridge with bottles.

Unfortunately, it will take longer for your beer to become carbonated when you put them in bottles. It usually takes a couple of weeks for the beer to condition properly in bottles. The level of carbonation may also be inconsistent from bottle to bottle. Bottling may also result in a small amount of sediment at the bottom of your beer. This sediment won't affect much, and some home brewers prefer it. But if you are hoping for a clean and clear finish, then kegging might be the way to go.

Another advantage of kegs is that they are easier to sanitize. You don't need a bunch of bottle caps when you move your beer into a keg. You can just siphon all of your finished beer directly into the keg. It's also much quicker for fermentation. Plus, the appeal of

DIY Home Beer Brewing For Beginners

drinking your own beer right out of the tap can't be overstated. Your friends will be impressed.

Kegs do take up more space, and they require special equipment. But kegging is more environmentally friendly. Kegging may not be the most practical choice for your first couple homebrewing projects, but it might be worth considering further down the line if brewing turns into a regular hobby.

How to Bottle Your Beer

Make sure to clean the inside of all of your bottles, especially if you are reusing old bottles. Then soak the bottles and the caps in your sanitizing solution.

Boil ¾ of a cup of corn sugar in two cups of water. Afterward, cover it up and let it cool down to room temperature.

DIY Home Beer Brewing For Beginners

Sanitize a bucket and put your priming sugar in it. Then siphon your beer from the secondary fermentation bucket into the bottling bucket. Siphoning is important because it keeps your beer from getting too stirred up and keeps sediment out of it.

Now that your beer has mixed with the sugar, it's primed. This is the last bit of food for the yeast, and what will eventually cause your beer to carbonate. Use the spigot on the bottling bucket to fill each bottle.

Place your bottles somewhere dark at room temperature. Someplace like the back of a closet will work. Leave it there for about two weeks for conditioning.

After two weeks, your beer is ready to drink! There will probably be a smaller layer of sediment at the bottom of the bottle. That is normal.

How to Keg Your Beer

DIY Home Beer Brewing For Beginners

The process for kegging will depend slightly on the type of equipment you have and the volume of beer that you have brewed. Because this is a beginner's manual, we assume that you will be bottling your first batch. But, in an effort to be as comprehensive as possible, we have added a list of equipment you will need for kegging and the basic steps required in the process. Be sure to consult the manual of whichever keg you decide to purchase.

You will need:

Keg

CO_2 tank

Regulator

Tap

Kegerator or refrigerator

DIY Home Beer Brewing For Beginners

Release pressure in the keg. Make sure you do this; it is a matter of safety.

Clean the keg of any debris or sediment from your last batch, and then use a solution to sanitize it.

Siphon your homebrew into the keg.

Seal your keg and pressurize it with CO_2, then place it in the refrigerator. You may need to slowly increase the pressure over the course of about a week.

Enjoy your homebrew, on tap.

Chapter 7: Common Issues And Troubleshooting

One of the best practices that you can do as a home brewer is to keep a detailed report of your brewing process. The more specific, the better. A minute-by-minute brew schedule and a journal of observations will help you learn and get the most out of each batch of beer. Remember that brewing is as much a science as it is an art, so be consistent and concise, so that if you brew something you like, you can repeat the recipe exactly as you did it the first time.

Mistakes are going to happen when you are learning any new skill or hobby. Brewing can take patience, and certain steps are more important than others. Adding an ingredient at the wrong time or forgetting to sanitize something may be detrimental to the beer you are trying to create.

DIY Home Beer Brewing For Beginners

If you keep detailed notes of your brew schedule, then when problems arise, you will have a much better way of figuring out the solution. Not only that, you will know which mistakes to avoid the next time you brew your own beer. Below is a list of very common homebrewing problems, what they mean, and how you can fix them.

Symptom: You pitch your yeast but after a few days, the airlock still isn't bubbling.

What it means: The worst-case scenario may be that your wort isn't fermenting. You could have gotten a bad batch of yeast, or maybe you didn't use enough yeast. Maybe the wort isn't the right temperature; it could be too hot or too cold. More likely than not, this problem actually has a very simple solution. There is a chance that your fermenting bucket isn't sealed properly. Before you go and try to buy more yeast, double check the seal on the airlock or on the lid to the bucket. Make sure the lid is on tight. It seems like 9/10 times, this is the cause of an airlock that hasn't started bubbling.

Symptom: Your beer tastes sour.

What it means: Your wort may have been contaminated. Maybe your mash got too cold during the mashing process. More than likely though, this is caused by contamination.

Make sure that you are sanitizing all of your equipment properly. This is probably the most important rule of brewing. If you are mashing your own grain, be sure to keep the mash at a consistent temperature.

Symptom: Your beer has a buttery flavor.

What it means: The yeast didn't completely absorb diacetyl. It could also mean your beer is contaminated. Remember to sanitize everything.

DIY Home Beer Brewing For Beginners

Symptom: Too many smells, too strong aroma.

What it means: It's possible that you fermented your beer at too high of a temperature or you didn't pitch the right amount of yeast. Try to ferment your next batch somewhere cooler, like your basement or in a dark closet.

Symptom: Your beer smells like band-aids.

What it means: Contamination. Remember the three S's of homebrewing: sanitize, sanitize, sanitize.

Symptom: Your beer smells or tastes vinegary.

What it means: Contamination. How many times do I have to say the word sanitize? It's possible that your beer could have been exposed to oxygen.

DIY Home Beer Brewing For Beginners

Symptom: Wort is too dark.

What it means: Your malt was too concentrated when you boiled it. It could have also been too hot during the boil.

Symptom: Final gravity is too high.

What it means: You used too much specialty grain or the wrong yeast strain.

Symptom: Not enough foam on the beer.

What it means: You didn't ferment enough, or there is not enough protein.

Symptom: Mold is growing on the top of your beer.

What it means: Might be caused by the yeast or exposure to oxygen.

DIY Home Beer Brewing For Beginners

Symptom: Beer is flat out of the bottle.

What it means: You need to condition the beer at warmer temperatures, or it needs to be conditioned longer. It's possible that the priming sugar was not mixed in well enough.

Symptom: Too much carbonation in the beer.

What it means: The priming sugar could be contaminated or not mixed right properly.

Symptom: Original gravity is too low.

What it means: You didn't add enough when topping up your wort.

Symptom: Beer has a cheesy smell/ flavor.

What it means: You used bad hops; either they were too old or stale.

DIY Home Beer Brewing For Beginners

Symptom: Beer tastes corny.

What it means: Wort cooled too slowly, contamination.

Symptom: Smells like nail polish.

What it means: You fermented the beer too much or there was not a good way for air to escape. The original gravity may also have been too high.

Symptom: Your beer tastes skunky.

What it means: Too much exposure to light. Try fermenting in a darker space. Did you use green or clear bottles? Make sure that you condition your beer in a dark place.

Symptom: Beer has a wet cardboard flavor.

DIY Home Beer Brewing For Beginners

What it means: The beer was exposed too late in fermentation.

Symptom: Too much sediment in the bottle.

What it means: You got too much sediment in when you siphoned it.

Symptom: Beer bottles are exploding (help!).

What it means: You used too much priming sugar, or the beer was bottled too early. There could also be too much gas from contamination. Sanitize!

Chapter 8: Beginner Beer Recipes

Traditional Hefeweizen Wheat Beer 4.5-5% ABV

For wheat beers, top-fermenting yeast is usually used. Wheat beers normally have very little hops, and they are light and refreshing. They make a good summer drink and can be enjoyed with most foods. Wheat beers are often a "gateway" beer for new craft beer drinkers, so for our first recipe, we've chosen a classic wheat beer called a Hefeweizen. This batch makes five gallons. There are a few more variations listed on the following page.

Ingredients:

Malts: 5 lbs. wheat DME or 6 lbs. wheat LME

DIY Home Beer Brewing For Beginners

<u>Specialty grains:</u> 1/2lb flaked wheat, ½ lb. flaked oats

<u>Hops:</u> 1 oz Hallertau bittering hop pellets

<u>Yeast:</u> White labs 300 hefeweizen yeast 3068 Weihenstephan

Directions:

Put two gallons of water in a pot and bring the water to 160 degrees Fahrenheit.

Put your specialty grains in a sack, and then steep for 60 minutes.

After 60 minutes, remove the grain.

Stir in your malt extracts.

DIY Home Beer Brewing For Beginners

Bring the wort to a boil.

Once the wort is boiling, add your bittering hops. Allow the wort to boil for 60 more minutes.

Cool the wort to room temperature as quickly as possible. Siphon the wort into your primary fermenter. Top off the wort so that it's about five gallons. Pitch the yeast and seal the bucket.

Fermentation should take about one week. After the bubbling in the airlock has slowed, move on to secondary fermentation or bottling.

Other things to try: Try adding special flavors to your beer. A few ounces of orange slices can be added during the end of the boil to give it a citrusy flavor.

DIY Home Beer Brewing For Beginners

Add about two pounds of tart, frozen fruit like strawberries, raspberries, or blueberries at the beginning of secondary fermentation.

DIY Home Beer Brewing For Beginners

American IPA 6.2% ABV

The IPA was originally created by the British to help beers last longer on long sea voyages. The natural antiseptic properties of the hops helped keep the beers from spoiling. The bitter flavor of the hops became popular as brewers began to experiment with different combinations of hops. Nowadays, the IPA has become a staple in the American craft beer movement.

Malts: 4.5lbs light DME, 3.3lbs Amber LME

Hops: 2oz Centennial, 2 oz Cascade

Yeast: American Ale Yeast Wyeast 1056

Directions:

DIY Home Beer Brewing For Beginners

Fill a pot with three gallons of water and add your malt extracts. Bring it to a boil.

Add 1 oz of Centennial hops and boil for 60 minutes.

Add 1 oz of Centennial hops and boil for 15 minutes.

Add 1 oz of Cascade hops at the end of the boil.

Cool the wort down to room temperature as quickly as possible. Siphon it into the primary fermenter. Top off the wort so that it reaches five gallons. Pitch the yeast and seal the bucket.

Let it ferment in the primary fermenter for one week. Move it into a secondary fermenter and add 1 oz of Cascade hops for aroma.

DIY Home Beer Brewing For Beginners

Leave the beer in the secondary fermenter for two weeks. Afterward, add priming sugar and transfer it into bottles. Let it sit for another two weeks before it is ready to drink.

Other things to try: Refer back to the list of hops earlier in this book. If you decide that the final product was not bitter enough or too bitter, remember the steps for calculating HBU. You can experiment with replacing the hops in this recipe to create your own kind of IPA.

DIY Home Beer Brewing For Beginners

Pale Ale 5% ABV

The pale ale is similar to the Indian Pale Ale in the use of hops to create a strong beer. Pale ales typically use paler, English style hops in order to balance the bitter flavor of the hops.

Ingredients:

Malts: 5.5lbs light DME

Specialty grains: 1/2lb Crystal 20L malt, crushed, 1/2lb American 6-row malt, crushed

Hops: 2 oz Centennial hops, 2 oz Cascade hops

11.5 grams of Safale dry yeast US-05

Directions:

DIY Home Beer Brewing For Beginners

Fill a pot with two gallons of water and heat to 160 degrees Fahrenheit. Place your specialty grains in a bag and steep for 20 minutes.

Remove the specialty grains from the pot.

Bring the water to a boil. While the water heats, slowly stir the malt extracts into the wort.

At the start of the boil, add ½ ounce of Centennial hops.

Let it boil for 45 minutes. Then add 1 oz of Cascade and 1 oz of Centennial hops by putting them in a nylon bag.

DIY Home Beer Brewing For Beginners

Let the wort boil for another hour. Remove the hops. Turn the stove off and move the pot off of the hot surface. Add another 1 oz of Cascade and ½ oz of Centennial into a new nylon bag.

Cool your wort to room temperature as fast as possible. After it has cooled, siphon it into the primary fermentation bucket. Pitch yeast and stir the wort.

Leave the beer to ferment for two or three weeks. When that is done, prime your beer with sugar and then bottle it. Let it condition in a dark place for another two weeks before it is ready to drink.

Other things to try: Use the pale ale as a way of experimenting with combinations of malts and hops. The right malt can balance the bitterness of the hops you choose, which is what pale ale is all about. Try steeping different malt combinations in hot water to test the flavor. Refer back to the flavor profiles and the HBU formula in order to create the perfect hop combination.

DIY Home Beer Brewing For Beginners

Amber Ale 4.5-5.5% ABV

Amber ales get their name because of their distinct color. They are similar to pale ales but typically use lighter malts.

Ingredients:

Malts: 3.3lbs Coopers LME, 3lbs amber DME

Specialty grains: 8oz crystal 40L, 2oz Crystal 135-165L

Hops: 2 oz Willamette hops, ½ oz Chinook hops

Yeast: White labs WLP001 California Ale yeast

¾ cup of priming sugar

Directions:

DIY Home Beer Brewing For Beginners

Put 3 gallons of water in a pot and bring it to 160 degrees Fahrenheit.

Put your specialty grains in a nylon bag and let it steep for 20 minutes.

Remove the specialty grains. Slowly stir in malt extracts.

Bring water to a boil. Add ½ oz of Chinook hops. Let it boil for 30 minutes.

After 30 minutes, add 1 oz of Willamette hops. Wait for 25 minutes and then add 1 oz of Willamette hops. Turn the stove off at 60 minutes and move the pot off of the hot burner.

DIY Home Beer Brewing For Beginners

Cool the wort to room temperature as quickly as possible. Top off the wort so that it reaches 5 gallons. Then, siphon it into the fermenter. Pitch the yeast and stir.

Seal the fermenter and let it sit for a week or so. After a week, move it to a secondary fermenter or prime it with sugar and bottle it.

Let it condition in a bottle for about two weeks before you drink it.

DIY Home Beer Brewing For Beginners

Porter 5-7% ABV

Porters are dark beers that tend to have a lot of flavors and are higher in alcohol content. They use dark specialty grains and brown malts to give the beer richness. They are very similar to stouts and were developed in London.

Ingredients:

Malts: 6.5lb light LME, 1lb Munich LME

Specialty grains: 1lb Crystal 40L malt crushed, 3/4lb Chocolate malt crushed, 1/2lb Black patent malt, crushed

Hops: 2oz Cascade hops

Yeast: 1lt started of liquid American Ale yeast

DIY Home Beer Brewing For Beginners

Directions:

Put 3 gallons of water in a pot. Put specialty grains in a nylon bag and increase the heat to 160 degrees Fahrenheit. Once the water reaches 160 degrees, remove the specialty grains.

Bring the wort to a boil. Stir the malts into the wort. Once the water starts to boil, add 1 oz of Cascade hops in a nylon bag.

Let the water boil for 45 minutes. Add another 1 oz Cascade hop to a nylon bag.

Turn off the stove at 60 minutes and move the pot from the hot burner. Bring the wort down to room temperature as quickly as possible. Siphon the wort

DIY Home Beer Brewing For Beginners

into the primary fermenter and top it off so that it reaches five gallons. Pitch your yeast and stir it in.

Let it age for 3-4 weeks before bottling. Let the beer condition in bottles for another 2 weeks before drinking.

Other things to try: Stouts and porters infused with coffee are very popular and hearty drinks. Brew some coffee and add it to your wort after you finish boiling or before you start secondary fermentation to give your beer more of a coffee flavor.

Conclusion

Hopefully, by reading this book, you will have begun to learn the tricks of brewing good beer right at home. There is a lot to learn, but practice makes perfect. The more beer that you brew, the more easily you will begin to understand the process and how all of the ingredients work together to make a delicious, malty beverage.

You don't need a lot of fancy equipment to make good beer. It is a very simple hobby that just requires a little understanding of science and a little creativity. Don't be intimidated by feeling like you have to fully understand the mechanics of each step or the flavor profile of each kind of hop. Start with one recipe at a time. Make a record of how each experiment affects the flavor of your beer. Some batches may turn out better than others. That is a normal part of learning how to brew beer at home.

DIY Home Beer Brewing For Beginners

These chapters should give you a good start, but also this book will serve as a good reference once you start to experiment with your own flavors. Start by choosing a recipe in the back and begin slowly making changes based on the flavor profiles for malts and hops that are provided. This is how you will start to create your own unique beers.

Erich M. Tolman

DIY Home Beer Brewing For Beginners

Connect with us on our Facebook page
www.facebook.com/bluesourceandfriends and stay
tuned to our latest book promotions and free
giveaways.

Printed in Great Britain
by Amazon